Brown Mouse
plays a trick

Story by Jenny Giles

Illustrations by Pat DeWitt-Grush

2

Gray Mouse said to Brown Mouse,
"I liked your party,
but I have to go home."

"I have to go home, too,"
said White Mouse.

4

Brown Mouse went to the door and looked out.

"You can't go home," he said. "The cat is outside the door."

6

"But we have to go home!"
 said Gray Mouse.

"Yes," said White Mouse.
"We will run fast."

"No!" said Brown Mouse.
"The cat will get you!"

8

Brown Mouse said,

"I will play a trick on the cat.

Look!

Here is my toy mouse.

My toy mouse looks like me."

"I will make my toy /100 mouse

run outside,"

said Brown Mouse.

"The cat will run after it,

and you can get home."

Brown Mouse

made the toy mouse run fast.

The cat looked at it.

The cat ran after the toy mouse.

Gray Mouse and White Mouse
ran home.

"I played a good trick

on the cat," said Brown Mouse.